This book belongs to...

....

LONDON, NEW YORK,
MELBOURNE, MUNICH, AND DELHI

Editor Charlie Gardner
Designer Fiona Gowen
Production Editor Melissa Latorre
Production Controller Jen Lockwood
U.S. Editor Jennifer Quasha

First published in the United States in 2009
by DK Publishing
375 Hudson Street
New York, New York 10014

09 10 11 12 13 10 9 8 7 6 5 4 3 2 1
175873—10/09

DK books are available at special discounts when purchased in bulk for
sales promotions, premiums, fundraising, or educational use. For details, contact:
DK Publishing Special markets
375 Hudson Street
New York, New York 10014
specialsales@dk.com

A catalog record for this book is
available from the Library of Congress.

ISBN: 978-0-7566-5836-6

Printed and bound in China by L-Rex

Discover more at
www.dk.com

The publisher would like to thank the following for
their kind permission to reproduce their photographs:

(Key: a-above; b-below/bottom; c-center; f-far; l-left; r-right; t-top)

Alamy Images: Alvey & Towers Picture Library 13tr; Mike Booth 7br; Imagebroker 15cr, 20cl; Yadid Levy 12-13, 18crb, 20tl;
LOOK Die Bildagentur der Fotografen GmbH 14, 18bl. Corbis: Kapoor Baldev / Sygma 15c; Reuters 15tr; Peter Turnley 8c. Denis Desmond: ltl, 8-9,
19tl, 20bl. DK Images: Rough Guides 6c (lamp post), 6c (red tree), 8fcl (red tree), lltr, 17cr (red tree). Getty Images: Mitchell Funk 10-11, 19br, 20br;
Robert Nickelsberg / Liaison 15cl; Taxi / Gary Buss 4cl; Taxi / Ken Chernus 5crb. iStockphoto.com: Nancy Louie 1br, 3, 4-5, 19cr, 20tr;
Joe Potato 16-17, 19cl; Rtyreel 5cra. Stickers: Alamy Images: Imagebroker c; Yadid Levy crb; LOOK Die Bildagentur der Fotografen GmbH clb.
Corbis: Peter Turnley cra. Denis Desmond: bl. Getty Images: Mitchell Funk tl. iStockphoto.com: Nancy Louie tr. Michael Perlman: cla.
Jacket images: Front: Alamy Images: Robert Harding Picture Library Ltd / Robert Francis. Back: iStockphoto.com: Nancy Louie t.

All other images © Dorling Kindersley

For further information see: www.dkimages.com

See how they go

Bus

Super school bus

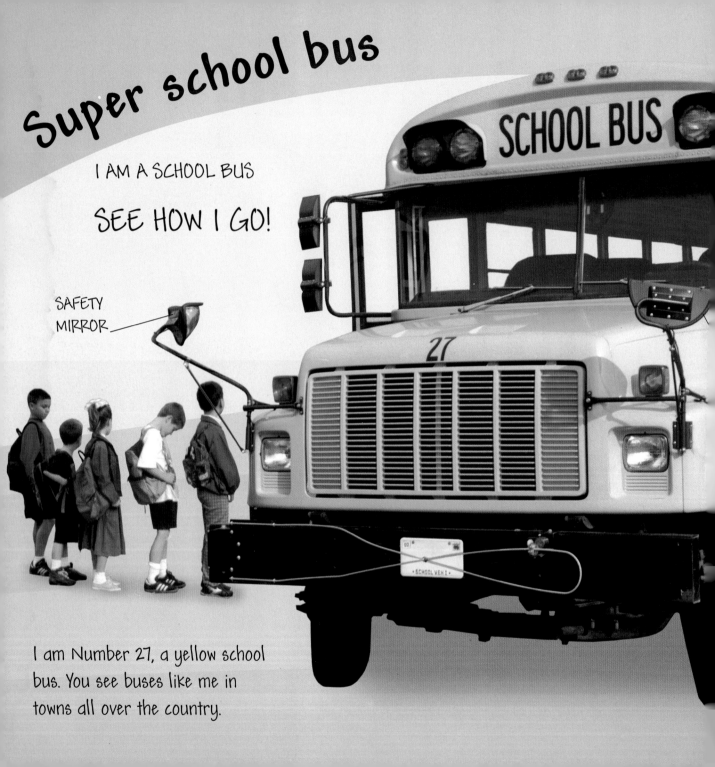

I AM A SCHOOL BUS

SEE HOW I GO!

SAFETY MIRROR

SCHOOL BUS

27

I am Number 27, a yellow school bus. You see buses like me in towns all over the country.

WARNING LIGHTS

Every school day, I leave early in the morning to pick up children and take them safely to school.

27

SAFETY MIRROR

FLIP-OUT STOP SIGN

In the afternoon, I wait at school ready to take the children back home. Do you know anyone who rides a school bus to school?

Double decker

I AM A DOUBLE-DECKER BUS

SEE HOW I GO!

I am a bus with seats upstairs. I can carry twice as many passengers as a single-decker bus the same length as I am.

DRIVER'S CAB

I have to be careful that my route doesn't include any low bridges. Do you know why?

TOP DECK

Upstairs on the top deck you get a great view. Buses like me are very popular for sightseeing. . .

TELEPHONE

ENTRANCE PLATFORM

Especially the open-top ones!

Bendy bus

I AM AN ARTICULATED BUS

SEE HOW I GO!

Look at me, I'm a bus that bends in half! My front and back are connected by a special swivel joint in my middle. This swivel makes me articulated, or flexible.

RUBBER CONCERTINAS

Can you see where the two ends of the bus join? Rubber curtains, or concertinas, keep it covered

AIR CONDITIONER

I am longer than a regular bus so I can carry more passengers.

FOLDING DOORS

Buses like me have lots of nicknames: accordion bus, banana bus, bendy bus, caterpillar bus, slinky bus. Do you know why?

Streetcar

I AM A STREETCAR

SEE HOW I GO!

I am part bus and part train. I run on railroad tracks just like a train. But I work on busy city streets where I stop and pick up passengers just like a bus.

WINCH CABLE

RUNNING BOARD

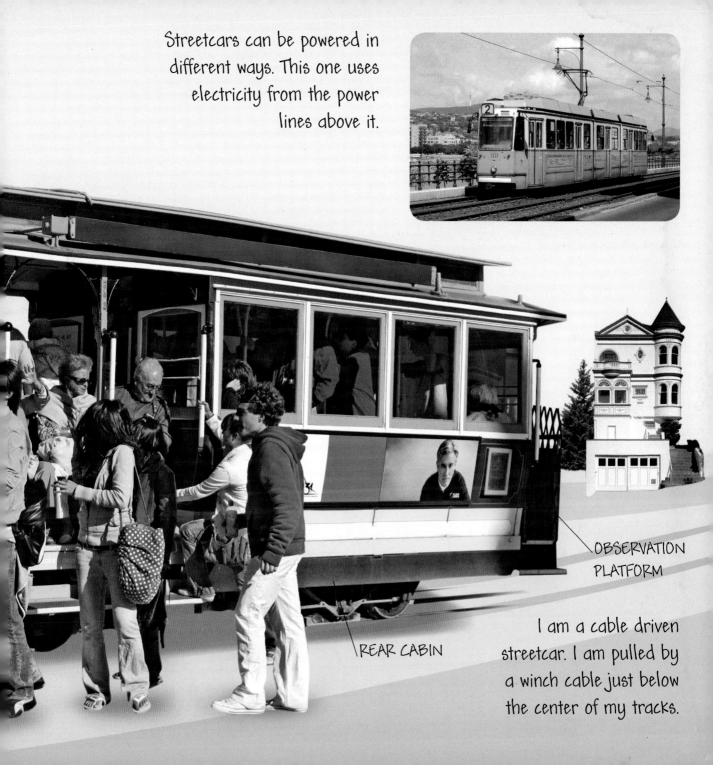

Streetcars can be powered in different ways. This one uses electricity from the power lines above it.

OBSERVATION PLATFORM

REAR CABIN

I am a cable driven streetcar. I am pulled by a winch cable just below the center of my tracks.

Electric bus

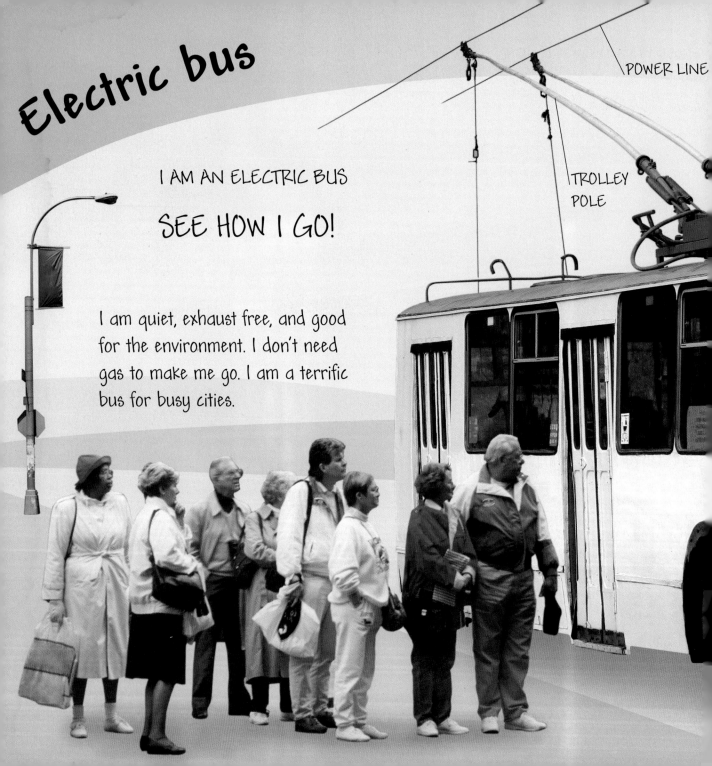

POWER LINE

TROLLEY POLE

I AM AN ELECTRIC BUS

SEE HOW I GO!

I am quiet, exhaust free, and good for the environment. I don't need gas to make me go. I am a terrific bus for busy cities.

I have two trolley poles that pick up electricity from the power lines above me.

The poles are longer than the type used on streetcars since I need more space to navigate wide roads.

SUN VISOR

4471

I also have batteries so that I can drive short distances on roads without cables.

Boutique bus

COLORFUL FLAGS

I AM A DECORATED BUS

SEE HOW I GO!

In some countries like Pakistan and the Philippines people decorate their buses by adding colors, decals, or special parts.

RAINBOW FRONT FENDER

Many buses and trucks in Pakistan are decorated both on the inside and the outside. Owners consider their buses to be works of art.

FLOOD LIGHTS

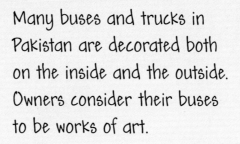

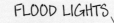

Jeepneys like me are a common sight in Manila, the capital of the Philippines. I am a jeep that has been made longer to hold more passengers. I love my bright paint work and shiny chrome!

Just like city buses in America, these colorful buses drive around picking up and dropping off riders.

Express bus

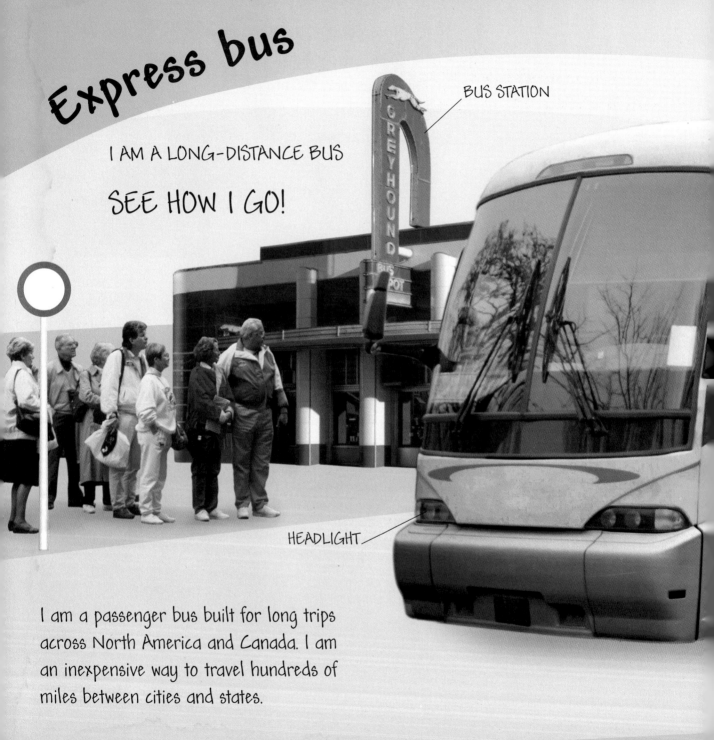

BUS STATION

I AM A LONG-DISTANCE BUS

SEE HOW I GO!

HEADLIGHT

I am a passenger bus built for long trips across North America and Canada. I am an inexpensive way to travel hundreds of miles between cities and states.

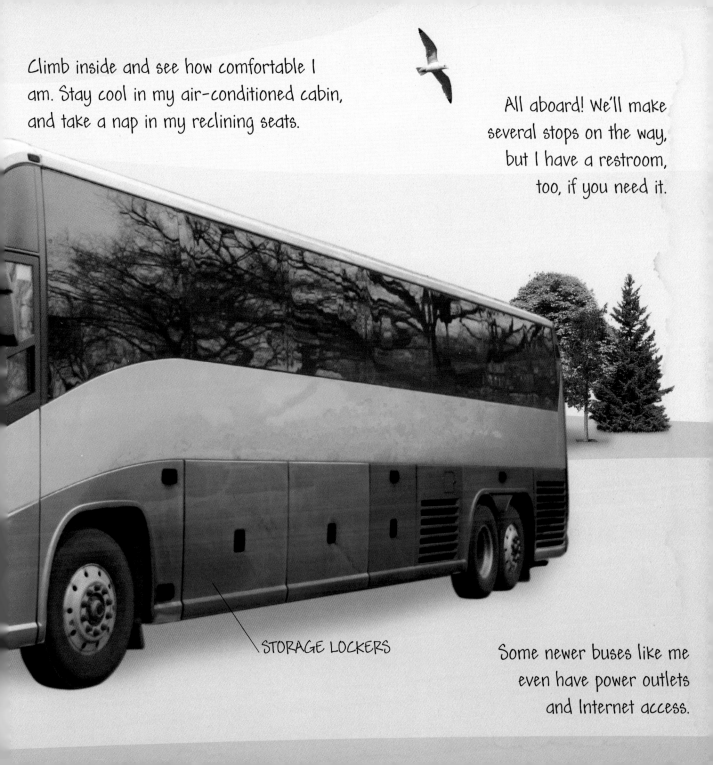

Climb inside and see how comfortable I am. Stay cool in my air-conditioned cabin, and take a nap in my reclining seats.

All aboard! We'll make several stops on the way, but I have a restroom, too, if you need it.

STORAGE LOCKERS

Some newer buses like me even have power outlets and Internet access.

See how they go!

Double decker

Electric bus

Jeepney

Articulated bus

School bus

Express bus

Streetcar

See How They Go!

Other titles:

Fire Truck
ISBN 978-0-7566-4553-3

Emergency Vehicles
ISBN 978-0-7566-5230-2

Train
ISBN 978-0-7566-4552-6

Boat
ISBN 978-0-7566-5522-8

Trucks
ISBN 978-0-7566-5168-8

Airplane
ISBN 978-0-7566-5521-1

Diggers
ISBN 978-0-7566-5167-1

Spaceship
ISBN 978-0-7566-5539-6

Cars
ISBN 978-0-7566-5231-9

Tractor
ISBN 978-0-7566-5540-2

Motorcycle
ISBN 978-0-7566-5838-0